Delight
Is a Field

Delight
Is a Field

poems by

Donelle Dreese

Karen George

Nancy K. Jentsch

Taunja Thomson

SHANTI ARTS PUBLISHING
BRUNSWICK, MAINE

Delight Is a Field

Published by Shanti Arts Publishing
Designed by Shanti Arts Designs

Cover image by pluie_r / shutterstock.com

Shanti Arts LLC
193 Hillside Road
Brunswick, Maine 04011
shantiarts.com

Printed in the United States of America

ISBN: 978-1-962082-69-3 (softcover)

Library of Congress Control Number: 2025938300

Contents

Angle

Jig

Ignite

Ascend

Ponder

Acknowledgments

Anthropocene: Poems About Environment: "Incessance"

Black Moon Magazine: "Star Song"; "Summer Solstice Magick"; and "The Watch"

Cultural Daily: "Afternoon Tea Daydreams"; "Clasped in a Moment of Fracture"; and "Winter Solstice"

The Field Guide Poetry Magazine: "Unshuttering"

Kentucky Philological Review: "Threadbare Day"

MacQueen's Quinterly: "The Moss-breasted Queen Luna"

Yearling: "Ascent"

Pavane

POSSIBILITIES

I am surrounded by courtiers
like so many sandhill cranes—
red-faced & bright-eyed, leggy,

trying for best foot forward,
dusky feathers for trains, crescent
moon curve of neck & back

with sun bouncing when gentle contour
turns to rambunctious snowy ridges
as they thrust-stroll beside me

like so many possibilities.
Years ago I walked out of a shack
brown & crumbling & hollow-eyed.

Now I always wear my best finery—
clouds for hat plumes, scarves knit
of the darkest soil & light as loam,

mossy sweaters, skirt with chiffon
sheen of snow, down to my boots—
tree trunks encrusted with the gems

of wind-whisked petal/grass stain/
leaf spine/ice shard. Yet I have decided
to set my crowing glory free—

that white peacock so like an unfolding
fan of fireworks that cool even while
sparkling & shimmying white hot.

I have taken the chain from his neck
& now we walk a wide field
with scarlet prospects, feathered spaces,

moonlit backbone & mouth full of sun.

Nancy K. Jentsch

THE WILES OF LOVE'S COURTIERS

Feathers are love's courtiers
proud as a strutting peacock whose eyes
graze on fields of flocking cranes.

They tickle, sly as snow
seduce veiled solemnity
into silliness, stoke quiversful

of wonder as awkward gait
shapeshifts into giddy flight.
They nick wind's wily sorcery

soaring past their conscience
that nods, drowsy as doomed
shack's sagging sashes.

Donelle Dreese

Haunted Shack among Cranes

The shack is mine, splinter of wood and soul
fire starter, ghost nest. I, once a farmer, now a bat
charmer, watch from a cracked roost, the gray
dimension I used to till. A woman, all white
feathered elegance, strolls and struts by in a sea
of pied piper sandhills. Her leashed peacock
sees me as a filthy orb floating, counting crimson
hats of cranes. The woman doesn't play the flute.
She hums, within the congregation of trills
and squawks, a song that dresses me in down.
Plumage pokes from my brain and breastbone.
My newborn neck stretches. I can finally fly home.

Karen George

THE MOSS-BREASTED QUEEN LUNA

holds court in a harvested cornfield
where her pages flock, hundreds of sandhill

cranes slate-gray, rusty undersides, crimson crowns.
Their queen looms, the marrow of their circle.

The ruffled alabaster plumage of her hat, collar, hair
matches the white peacock she walks on a leash.

The waterfowl preen, titillate, placate with dance:
bow, leap, staccato wing flap, the cadence

accompanied by trills and purrs that echo
through bleak autumn air. She carries a scepter,

crest a shock of quills and thistles. Or is it a riding crop
to maintain distance, keep the fray and their stiletto

bills away? She shuns the bare, tilted oak, the ashen
farmhouse—her birthplace—riddled with secrets.

Parade

Karen George

REDHEADED QUEENS OF THE MARSHLAND

We carry our cattail scepters high like torches,
survey our riparian queendom to plot
our autumnal equinox.

We slosh ankle-deep water, golden swamp
grasses swish our hips. A merl
of red-winged blackbirds

jounces crowns of cattails pecked open
to plunder fuzzy white down
to soften cup-shaped nests

trussed to vertical stalks' stout bases. Soon
we'll harvest tender lower shoots
for salads, dry reeds to weave

mats, baskets, hats; seed fluff to stuff pillows
and quilts, insulate coats, stunt bleeding,
amass sap to heal wounds.

Each flowerhead yields 250,000 seeds.
Some we grind into flour, many
we sow, the rest preserve

in seed banks. And O, under the harvest
moon, around the fire, we'll feast,
sing, dance, drum.

Taunja Thomson

SEPTEMBER'S PARADE

Two women march through a windy autumn day
on which sky has cast itself smoke & pearl.

The field around them waves grasses
the color of spelt as high as their hips.

The woman in front wears her spun gold hair
like a messy halo. The other has donned

a black dress, white lace collar, & an apron
peppered with faded mauve flowers.

Both carry cattails, stem, sprout, spike, flower,
& fluff, as if they are staffs, as if a long line

of people followed them, gilded fanfare, acrobats
leaping over bulls, a patchwork of reds & blues.

Yet wind sweeps the field, the only sound its scrape
against branch & shoot & the two women's

bodies. The only accompaniment sits bobbing on cattails,
weighing them down—red-winged & yellow-headed

blackbirds, tails out, heads up. The women's destination
is unknown to anyone but them. They follow

an invisible line, a silent call. The visible?
Their grim mouths & stone faces, stoic against

equinox gusts.

Nancy K. Jentsch

THE WATCH

Process with me through this drumbeat dream
silvered march across fantasy's acres
lit by singing cattail tapers.

Pamper legs with second-skin tights
like boots standing guard between creek
and legs, between being in and one with the wind.

Walk past birds budding choruses
of plumage led by heron's baton beak.
Let these choristers be not merely meadow's

random buttons, but storied threads that weave
a coverlet telling of blackbirds' longing
the scuffed sky's yawn, recounting

so much more than the simple
sum of dream's clamoring parts.

FUR

A weight of wild fog is lifting.
Its wet fur releases, shifts as a polar
bear rising from slumber. We are all
hungry, looking for the unclouded.
A blackbird choir—yellow-headed,
red-winged, angel-footed—begins
its solar song with throats as open
windows. Cattails rocket skyward
as fur torches, sun seducers, mist
piercers. Even the blonde grass purrs
like fur, a buttered rug, still spreading.
What the women want you to know
is this—they see radiance and are
bringing it home.

Return

Karen George

SIMMERING

On the kitchen windowsill, one pie cools, another's
crust fluted, fitted in place against the tin,
a smatter of apple slivers arranged.

A man's black hat hangs on
the chair stile's ear. In the yard, a murder
of crows shrieks and swoops. Sheer, gauzy curtains

puff and flutter from the open window. A woman
wears a lacy, deep V-neck dress, apron
cinched around her waist. Her rump

leans on the table, hand wedged against
its hard, sharp edge and the fact that *the apple
of her eye* will not return—just foretold by the hoary

crow. Hornets gash the bubbly crust, suck limp
fruit. On the rolling pin, one lands, prods
raw dough lumps. A yellow jacket

alights on the tender crook of her
elbow, jabs its stinger past her skin. Two
wasps roost near her stricken heart. Her dark

eyes narrow, glare, pierce. Her rigid face
shines with sweat, ginger hair
a thick jolt of revolt.

Her wrist hums,
grazes the handle—
the abandoned knife.

Donelle Dreese

CONFESSIONS

Crow flight over wisp of wheat.
Swarm of wasp and wind.
Green apple peels, flour-dusted.

He'll be home soon.
His hat waits on the chair
draped, drunk and lazy.

Curtain sheers flip and fold
above piping pastry fog
aromatic crust and core.

I'm not afraid of bee stings
or gray, tart afternoons
fingers buttery and baked out.

Two dirt tracks form a road,
one that I could crumb-drizzle
but I stay for the confession

the way his eyes become
orchards when he inhales
love in the latticework.

Nancy K. Jentsch

TREADMILL

From dream's rickety treadmill
she views creeks whose flowing
sleeps, eternal swarms of bugs,
tired slogs knee-deep in bogs
of molasses, an apple pie
shelved and ever waiting
for baking and sharing.

Even as dreams tread on
the apples of her eye taunt
just beyond her grasp—wasp-free
hour, harvest's earthy perfume,
prize-worthy pie crust, cheek
raised to solstice breeze, return
of black cap's wandering owner.

OPALED

I am the apple of my eye—not
slick red with sun's wash or bumpy
yellow with matte finish. No,
I am green—a field raging

with wind-and-switchgrass melee
& the lone cottonwood spindled
with blooms that hover over
the ruckus below. I am

a shamrock apple—skin & stem
& seed & pulp & core—a heart
split in two & a whole orb
in the same space. I can be

plucked by the hand of universe
thrown to ground   rolled downhill
stomped by foot   broken by ant
mandibles   cut up   laid

on a table with rain blowing
in kitchen windows & sprinkling me
with cold slivers or sun lancing
its way through skylight

& onto my thick husk. Wasps
can slip through door ajar & brood
in corners until they come calling
& land on me. It doesn't matter—

I cast my moss/pine/spinach/sea
complexion onto their pointed
torsos/antenna/& even their eyes
through windows & out to tide

of tall grass with its tree rising
like a reef bustling with birds the colors
of anemone & just as hungry.
I even patina the wings of crows

who dive into the depths of field
& rise with beetles gleaming like scarabs—
sacred & filling—in their barbed beaks.
At that moment between this world

& the next even those shells shine
like apples—opaled   green electric   cosmic.

Alight

LIGHT

Strip away the layers of daylight—
cars' ticking thrum   rush of feet
crush of voices   buildings' sharp
shadowed edges. Strip all this

then dismantle your own smile
the one you fasten to your face
undo your busy hands   let them
fall to your sides   annihilate

desire   that puppeteer jerking
your legs along concrete avenues
extinguish chains of syllables
careening down tracks—trains

spewing words that curl & vanish.
Now relax your mouth   from back
of throat send a hum down spine
feel it uncoil in a sun of your own

making   a corn snake basking.
With a thought conjure a cool
moon on your brow   realize
the whiteness of your skeleton—

knitted ribs   woven knees   tatted
fingers   simple as stars   clean as night.
Open your eyes   watch moths land
on your sternum & braid themselves

into a fleecy fluttering collar
that kisses your neck. Contemplate
fireflies against lilac bush—a darkling
crone bending her way toward you.

Open your mouth so they can skate
down throat   spangle your frame.
Now you light your own way
jaw   ear   hip   sole.

Donelle Dreese

ALIGHT

What is the difference between star and firefly?
Nothing, nocturne flickers. Both are bellies
of solar memory, creative fire. I unchurch myself
from factory and tower for crickets and peepers
in black ponds, and moth footprints on a blouse
of lace and lily, and for trees lost in their own wood
pulp surrounded by surprise and blink. Fireflies
are soft stars you can hold in your hand, alight
bodies of alchemy, and stardust is elemental
in the warm navy narrative of the midnight sky.
If tomorrow's nightfall is this showy, you come too.
Bring your mystery.

SUMMER SOLSTICE MAGICK

Stars speckle midnight-blue heavens,
echo fireflies' flit against tree silhouettes

and green-black grass. Framed by that tapestry,
a female in sheer white pleated voile edged

in lace, sleeves curved like clam shells
the shade of champagne, an ivory cloche hat

with tulle netting and a large silver brooch
set with swirls of diamonds. Copper hair

pulled back, one loose tendril—an antenna.
Her pale face a reflection of the full moon,

luminous, dreamy as a Chopin nocturne.
Whisper-light moths land on her hat, ear, collar,

shoulder, pocket: sphinx, gypsy, skipper, silk.
Her dark eyes loom directly at you, mouth

a flirt-smile, lips clasping a secret. Moths sip
from her dewy skin powder-soft as their wings.

Did she molt, moments ago, from a cocoon
into this goddess, priestess, bride, queen?

STAR SONG

Night is a woman veiled
in star song, her brocade
is horizon's twilight outline
her lips a crescent sliver.

Night invites insect hands
to play Chopin; their fans
tempt Fate like moths
till Fate wins. Fireflies

ignite theater's backdrop
warm drafty corners
with their lust, their hushed
pleading. When dawn

closes curtain on night's
waning face, musicians exit
stage right, sunlight
blinding their song.

Delight

Taunja Thomson

DELIGHT IS A FIELD

where gamagrass waves ripple & crackle
with orange stamen & purple stigmas

& creamsicle edges in autumn. Delight
is a field in which I sit on a blanket

while wind ferries the scent of wet soil
up to a solid grey sky & hurls my hair

over my head, never allowing it to settle
slick & calm over my ears. Delight strolls

over to me like a white goat & nudges
my arm for cinnamon tea & zucchini bread.

Delight perches like a lone tree in the distance
leaning against a horizon spinning a storm

like a saga of cloud & clover   hill & blade
a tale that starts in a bead of rain & ends

glistening on my shoulders under their thin
cotton & running down my striped stockings

& around my red Mary Jane's. Delight is a field
clattering with crowspeak—rusty & creaking

like unpolished, unoiled doors of current
& veer   dip & dive   velocity & drift.

Donelle Dreese

EARL GREY AFTERNOON

This wounded world
golden layered landscape
lean of wheat and ivory goat
has two green apples
one for me
one for you
both of us bedded down
in bullrush and sweetgrass
on an Earl Grey afternoon
post-torrent
post-talk.
The biscuits are knitted
with chrysanthemum petals
and the goats have decided
they like us
they join us
here in some lost prairie
brittle with grasshopper bones
a cricket's life
a lady-bug's life.
Dream big, the hills say.
The only tree visible for miles
will show you how.

Nancy K. Jentsch

Twin(s)

Our legs seek sun on a flannel blanket—
teatime in a field of ripening oats.

I wear a pink shirtwaist;
I wear a blue shift.

I choose shoes for comfort;
I buy pointy-toed boots.

I am my own fraternal twin.

I sip tea, dreamily serene;
I frown, puzzled by the cosmos.

Two unbitten apples tempt
invite us to mischief.

I'm pleased with tea;
I'll proceed to Eve's downfall.

Karen George

Afternoon Tea Daydreams

In the hilly pasture, my twin sister and I sit
on dense Irish damask (white with swirls
pearly as oyster shells) Granny handed down

along with her farm, shamrock china, and the art
of reading tea leaves. Deidre hands me a cup
of Merlin's Magic Elixir of Life ordered

from Galway, mélange of lemon myrtle,
marigold petals, grapes, rosehip peels.
She overflows her cup from the pewter

kettle, in a reverie of last summer's lover.
We've spread homegrown cucumbers
with our goats' cheese seasoned

by rosemary and thyme. Kaylie joins us,
mouth sunk in the cream crock we filled for her,
eyes drowsy—*milk drunk* we call it—daydreams

of suckling her nanny's teat only a year ago.
The feral smell of her fur mixes with whiffs
of seaweed shampoo from our wind-frizzed

auburn hair. The sun's heat on my back,
the rhythmic lap of tongue, and the sigh
of dry ryegrass tilts me into a nap.

Angle

Auburn

A dog, auburn, with touch
of chocolate, delivers a fish

from its saltwater mouth
to a hand, blushed with cold.

Sweep, swing, and spray
of indigo sea touches the sky

gray-layered with autumn's
trail of howling vapor.

Ripe grasses, course as hay
hold a woman, also auburn

with lace collar and sunflower skirt.
Her braid entwines the bond

between woman and wolf—
an infinite, auburn, embering love.

It calls on the driftwood shoreline
as a bark wrapped in mist

while the fish arcs and drips
away the slick memory of its life.

INCESSANCE

Earth tones upstage ocean's cresting green
Hair wisps, imitates waves' raging foam
interrupts day's stormy horizon

Dog and mistress trade timid glances
Unspoken reactions ignore
sea's brutal incessance

But bound by rings of ruffled droplets
by open eyes, measured breaths
triangle of dog, woman, fish

will expire while sea collects days, years
centuries, millennia in its infinite
album of bountiful chaos

Karen George

CLASPED IN A MOMENT OF FRACTURE

Her spaniel Vincent, returned from an ocean plunge,
releases a snatched mackerel into the woman's open palm.
She wants no part of what her delicate fingers support—
this limp, opal-scaled body, its rheumy eyes gone dark. Her
eyes distant, she chafes the past and future. Vincent's wise
gaze fixes on a sandpiper hopping ahead. The fur on his
ears, the tawny amber of honey, and her plush chestnut hair
blow askew in high winds. He's collarless; she wears a white
ruffle around her neck that echoes a silver choker. Saltwater
droplets from the fish and dog's mouth mirror the crystal
rosary beads she fingered last night to find an answer. A
blustery sky and waves arched in ecstasy frame her face,
pearly as moonlight.

SHALLOWS

Fetch my heart out of the brine—
it beats with a rasp now
because rocking
against reefs

in the sway of tide has roughened
it up. Sharks' teeth imprinted
themselves on valve
& vein. Remora

tried to pick it clean for a polished
sheen but only succeeded
in drying it out
& leaving it

desiccated. The salt & foam have
infiltrated aorta's arch leaving
it the palest of reds
& stringy.

Now you bring my heart to me in all
its brackish ignominy—dripping
& flopping as if it is a fish
& air its mortal

enemy. I want to throw it back
& let the moon-laden tide
drag it out to rest
in a forest

of kelp in the cool but sun-stoked
shallows. Let sea stars grope
for footholds & creep
among my atria.

Let jellyfish float nearby like lamps
let anemone tickle ventricle
let otters hide from storm
let gulls dip

& dine. Let sharks gleam & glide
& prowl like midnights
given shape & dark
definition.

Leave my heart in the shallows—
depths tumble me tigerishly
& breeze parches
artery.

Jig

SONGBIRD SISTERS

A storm whistle blows on the horizon.

Violin grief is the most potent
of all, but the gulls are hungry

and the house is dark with only
a single flutter of its lacy hand.

It's time to eat cake and burn
the candelabra before the seaweed

wind turns dune grass into sorrow sand.
Let smoking points of fire poke holes

in the slate sea spray and let the dog
devour the fresh bowl of cherries.

The songbird sisters are not afraid
of mornings of melody and discord.

They dance while a white gull
picks meat from dead crab bones.

They drink coffee on a grainy shoreline
in a world that is a cosmology of debris.

Nancy K. Jentsch

WILD DANCE

A cape is a jut of land
out of place—tongue
wagging tut-tutting tales
an oil rig's profits sickening
fishes' ancestral pool
a meat-hungry dog
clawing Granny's lace
a left-handed fiddler
tempting tunes from wood.

A cape seethes danger—
finger pointed like gull's
greedy beak luring undertow's
sleight of hand and row
after row of foaming breakers
under clouds' inky pigment.

A cape tempts its guests—
their feet kick off well-shined
shoes to share its booty
be seduced by wild dance
of tides and jig in time
with wind's whimsy.

THREE COUSINS PLAN THE FUTURE

Intent on outcomes, the trinity pulls out
scarred kitchen table, mismatched chairs
from their 150-year-old ancestral home

on Cape Cod's shore. Tax debt and disrepair
continue to accrue since their last aunt, Keily,
passed five years ago. Irish lace covers the table,

is knotted at Orla's throat, billows from glassless
windows, curtains frothy as nearby whitecaps.
They've finished lunch, but not their discussion.

Auburn-haired Imogen plops her two potbelly pigs
on the table to slop leftovers. Her black pug grabs
an iced Guinness cake from her plate. A gull swoops,

snatches the lobster carcass, drops it in parched
grass, its beak rasping as it stabs past the hard shell.
Wind howls, seizes their long hair, snuffs lit flames

of a three-armed candelabra, settles salty sea mist
on their skin. When talk turns tense, blonde Orla
picks up her fiddle, launches into Swallowtail Jig,

vies with screeches of circling gulls and pig snorts,
grunts, wet lip-smacks. Redheaded Shannon can't resist
the rhythmic tune. Head high, torso rigid, hands on hips,

she springs into breakneck dance steps, her full circle skirt
flares out from her body. Music and dance quicken, usher
in the imminent storm. Nothing's resolved. Imogen's vexed,

taut as the fiddle's steel strings, ready to snap.

METAMORPHOSIS

The cape of ocean—blue-black with spume for lace—
    rocks in a wind
that descends from the tawny sky riddled with electrum clouds.

Seagulls pursue each crash that yields dung & berries
    & silvered herring
& mackerel with fins sharp as sails, some wriggling, some still.

Hem of sea's cape almost touches old house tarnished sepia
    by mistral/
fog/spray, & filigreed curtains sneaking out window flap
    & mirror the ghost

bird that roosts on eave—jet black with white lightning
    down his neck
& a crest of crimson, an arrow, a blaze, a flicker of what
    once was.

The women have abandoned that box of beds & tea & telephones
& *will you have some more/yes thank you/welcome.* They wait

for that aquatic cloak to cover them so that they will never
    be cold again,
never shiver, never gasp in surprise, never exhale with laughter.

In the meantime, they dance to a demon fiddle, & their dogs
    assault a table
laid with opal apples/red velvet cake/violet grapes/chiffon
    pie/spinach

as round as linden leaves & as green as weeping willows.
    They twirl
& bob, ballet & writhe under a close sun, dressed in their
    new indigo finery—

a poncho of waves & reef, ebb tide, neap tide—woman & dog.

Ignite

THREADBARE DAY

When lit, fingers of wood
lift chill morning's fog
heat threadbare days

flame auburn like wisps
of wind-waltzing hair
till night tucks in

black as crowding crows.

Lithe fingers that once reached
like kite strings to sky's
infinity now serve

only this day's purposes
clutched close to pulsing heart.

Karen George

WINTER SOLSTICE

The first snowstorm melted except
for a patch by the barn where the family

of five crows swooped from their roost
after I threw dry kibble our Corgi refused

to eat. Their caws and wings percuss air.
I swish through fields, flatten russet crests

of ryegrass, gather branches. Fog entwines
birch trunks, ghosts the barn, soot-black

with age. Wind and cold chap my cheeks
and lips. Soon as dark descends, my love

returns. We'll howl around flames,
revel in heat, color, crackle, spark,

launch our hibernation.

ENDINGS

I was not expecting it. Autumn sat,
crisp & misty, around me—in the boughs
of oak, in the brown grass at my feet,
in the black sheen of raven wings.

I held the pale sticks of wood
to my chest as I traipsed through field,
breathed in the wet cool air, & looked forward
to the crackle of fire, the flying of embers,

the stamping of feet & the rubbing together
of hands, blowing on them with cold lips. Then
it happened—wind rose & circled me,
lifting hair & chafing face.

I saw the dusk-hued smoke rising
from the shack up ahead, the one I thought
was mine. Its sharp edges blurred in a fire not
of my making, its roof sprouted holes,

that door melted shut. I dropped kindling,
arms, & love in one breath, pulled my coat & scarf
tighter, turned, walked back the way I came—
through a field shadowed by oak,

peppered by mushroom,
punctuated by croaks of ravens
as they sailed to the next field frosted with fall
& a hope for warmth.

Donelle Dreese

THE INGATHERING

So little to burn
when the goodbye barn
stands like cold charcoal
enfolded in a steel fog
smoke quilt of morning
as hunger ravens
locate their first kill.
On the russet prairie
fire isn't always for heat.
Sometimes it's for igniting
a will to live, one bare-boned
branch at a time while the gold
blood of sun fails to bloom.
What the solstice sky
willingly withholds,
sleeping oaks offer up
in bundles and bonfires,
the shape of stick and staff,
an ingathering of twig
and timber pressed close
to the chest like a locket
or a love.

Ascend

STARLINGS FOLLOW ME

When alone in the easy winter of my own making,
I am a snow field covered in spotted starlings.
At night, the spots dance away in speckled union
to join a confluence of galaxies somewhere
between cortex and deep space, artery and cloud.
When I unbutton my coat, a starling flies out to feed
on a sunflower seed trail left behind by an old love.
It emerges from my floral skirt like a black dove
to remind me of his feathered hands. Starlings
follow me in murmuration, tugging at my winged
scarf to keep going, pushing me toward unison.
I am always in flight even if you can't see it.

Unraveling, Unleashed

The wind lifts a woman's knitted black and white scarf,
     splits it in a vee, unravels the yarn into a wave

of ten thousand starlings headed for an unclad tree.
Her auburn hair, a swirl of braids, floats like thick

liquid smoke. With one gloved hand she holds
a long plaid coat close, a swung-open flap reveals

the flounced skirt of a dark flowered dress
where a bird hovers, just released

from the fabric's folds. One pecks
swirling snow near her high-buttoned boots,

another threatens to grasp her coat hem
in its unlatched beak, to pluck her

into the squalling vault.

Ascent

Dressed for solstice climb
boots riveted in blown snow
steel gray and chain-mail helmeted

she begins: exhales frayed
energy cloudward as stresses
unbraid, tresses towering proud.

She pinches and lifts coat's
corner to unlock what flocked
within. Starling invaders unfurl, ascend

in synchronous flight to chide
horizon's leafless silhouettes. Not
even cackling stragglers distract her ascent.

SUMMER ONCE

I was dealt a hand of ravens   a hand
of snow. One hand folded into wings

of viridian   the other drifted
into powder beneath my booted

feet. Even in my summers
I could hear their croaks

& grunts. Under June
suns my feet froze—

I could not move forward.
I could not emerge
from (fore)shadow(ing).

Now my feather-hand flies
through afternoons   roosts

under moons   weaves a sheen
of light in all things. My flurry-

hand soothes forehead   insulates
against fever-thoughts. Murmuration

follows me   dips & braids & utters my will
as I raven the pulsing stream of marrow

that summer once withheld.

Ponder

UNSHUTTERING

She ponders hollow bones
their lift and glide, soar
and swoop, gray-
shingled wings arching
to befriend air currents.
She squints as birds
of the air crisscross,
their DNA scribbled
with scripture. Her musings
fledge, thread her into
densest cacophony—
kitty-waaking that revives
her shuttered spirit
nudges her cobwebbed soul.

Karen George

SEARCHING FOR SOLACE

I long to feel close to Granny Gisele as when I lived with
her the summer I turned five: honey-blond hair, long braids
coiled in a chignon snugged on the nape of her neck, or
hugging her head, a golden crown. I accompanied her
to Sunday services, back when faith was a refuge: sweet
smiles of church ladies, songs that made my body purr like
Granny's tabby Helga.

I leave the graveside ceremony, find the abandoned church
still perched on the hill's crest that slopes down to the sea:
a once white, now ashen clapboard with black roof—stained
glass windows and bronze bell long gone.

The sun's beefy heat, the gulls' shrieks pierce, dizzy me. On
my back in parched beachgrass more yellow than green, I
inhale the briny, raw sea scent, note a hint of thunderstorm.
I shade my eyes with the back of my hand, palm open to
eclipsed sky, my hair a dark frizzed cloud.

To clear my mind, I focus on the surf's endless collapse, try
to rise above the muck. A large gull hovers above me, its
shadow and the underside of its wings the reek, the squeeze
of grief.

REFUGE

Belfry has been rumbling
forever, but where
are the bats?

I've longed for their frosted backs
& dark bellies, those orange spots
behind each curled ear, pined
for leather wings wrapped
around them like inky capes,
cauldron of conks lining caves
of mind.

But they are not here. Instead,
a bedlam of bells shrieks
in tower.

Past time to leave & step out
into a field under sky marbled
pewter/slate/charcoal & avowing
rain, so here
I go.

No bats, but olive-gold grass capers
in susurrus of wind, shimmy & sway
with ballet interlude inviting me
to sit a spell, to utter a spell
that brings the winged down
to me.

And down they come, seagulls riding
rushes of gust, bills the color of sun
& ajar with *huoh huoh huoh*, whiteboard
wings & tail feathers of flint
echoing sky.

They waft over to church, envelope black
tower/steep roof/tarnished siding/
dark windows.

The rest sail over me to & fro, to
& fro until toes/hips/torso/scalp
drift over sage sward, seedhead
tickling spine.

Now thunder ripples through me,
raindrops sprinkle skin, distant
blaring bells silent in thrum
of bird call.

And I know that as day strides
forward & dives into the purple
stains of twilight, that cloud
of brown bellies & jet
wings & vibrato warbling
will descend in lovely
crepuscular throes

my own tremolo heart beating
a wide rhythm in this field
straddling a span of unfurled
sky & glinting blades
& wings spun in storm's
bracing trundle.

HOLY FLOCK

This prairie is my bed of extraordinary sighs.
I exhale the world here. Life's daily vapors.
Each little loss is a stone that rolls away
until a seagull claims it with her crone claws.
A great worry thief, she tucks it into the sky
until the clouds cry out pebbled nightmares
as hail. A passerine wind over prairie grass lifts
a holy flock of birds circling a church. A ghost
sermon rises from the steeple. I don't remember
when I last touched a poppy or saw a crocus poke
through snow, but the sermon is about flowers,
rebirth, resurrection, our reliance on death
as a seed, not a subtraction. Maybe I will lie
here until a thousand tentacles of grass turn me
into tiny button mushrooms and meadow hair.

ABOUT THE AUTHORS

DONELLE DREESE is a writer and Professor of English at Northern Kentucky University where she teaches environmental and multicultural literatures, American women poets, and literature and film. Donelle is the author of several poetry collections, including *Sophrosyne* (2015) and *Organelle* (2021). Her poetry and essays have appeared in a wide variety of literary journals, including *Potomac Review*, *Roanoke Review*, *Louisville Review*, and *Quiddity International*. In addition, Donelle serves as President of Heritage Acres Memorial Sanctuary, Cincinnati's only dedicated natural burial preserve. She writes about natural burial and "death positive" topics as a regular contributor for *Psychology Today*. For more information, visit donelledreese.com.

KAREN GEORGE is a retired programmer/analyst and author of five chapbooks, most recently the collaborative ekphrastic *Frame and Mount the Sky* (Finishing Line Press, 2017) and four poetry collections: *Swim Your Way Back* (2014), *A Map and One Year* (2018), *Where Wind Tastes Like Pears* (2021), and *Caught in the Trembling Net* (2024). She has received grants from Kentucky Foundation for Women and Kentucky Arts Council. She won Slippery Elm's 2022 poetry contest, and her award-winning short story collection, *How We Fracture*, was published by Minerva Rising Press in 2024. Her work appears in *Adirondack Review*, *Valparaiso Poetry Review*, *Ekphrastic Poetry Review*, *Indianapolis Review*, *Salamander*, and *Poet Lore*. For more information, visit karenlgeorge.blogspot.com.

NANCY K. JENTSCH is a retired German professor at Northern Kentucky University. Her chapbook *Authorized Visitors* (Cherry Grove Collections) and the collaborative ekphrastic chapbook *Frame and Mount the Sky* (Finishing Line Press), in which her poetry appears, were published in 2017. Since 2008, when she began writing, her work has appeared in both online and print journals, such as *Amethyst Review*,

Eclectica, *Panoply*, *Tiferet Journal*, and *Zingara Poetry Review*, and also in numerous anthologies. In 2020 she received an Arts Enrichment Grant from the Kentucky Foundation for Women. Her collection *Between the Rows* was published by Shanti Arts in 2022 and a chapbook, *Intersecting Orbits* (Bottlecap Press), in 2024. For more information, visit jentsch8.wixsite.com/my-site.

TAUNJA THOMSON is a former Northern Kentucky University English instructor, with many interests, including mythology, anthropology, history, art, and animal rights. She is a co-author of the chapbook *Frame and Mount the Sky* (Finishing Line Press, 2017) and author of chapbooks *Strum and Lull* (Plan B Press, 2019) and *The Profusion* (Kelsay Books, 2019). Her poetry has appeared in many journals over the years, including *Peacock Journal*, *Pink Panther Magazine*, *These Fragile Lilacs*, *Red-Headed Stepchild*, and *Quillkeeper's Press*. Her full-length poetry collection, *Plunge*, was published in 2023 by Raw Art Review. For links to her published poetry, visit www.facebook.com/TaunjaThomsonWriter.

www.ingramcontent.com/pod-product-compliance
Lightning Source LLC
Chambersburg PA
CBHW071356090426
42738CB00012B/3134